SECRETS OF GOLF

(FOR WOMEN ONLY)

BY

MAGGIE GREEN

LUV

M

SECRETS OF GOLF

(FOR WOMEN ONLY)

BY

MAGGIE GREEN

DRAWINGS

BY

RAY RUSSOTTO

THE OUTLINE

THE INTRO

Here I am:

I have been working on my game….

I have been taking lessons….

I have had wonderful pros;

I have had terrible pros.

I have worked on every aspect
  of this game.

I have had shoulder surgery.

I have had back surgery.

I have had tendonitis.

I have suffered through OLD AGE

(**50** + + +)

I have had wonderful partners
 and friends;

Some are great golfers....

Some are awful golfers.

Some love lessons;

Some hate lessons.

Some struggle (like me).

Some do not.

BUT we all have this in common:

We all get frustrated.

We all get upset.

We all feel superior.

We all feel inferior.

We all cry,

We all laugh,

We all………..

LOVE THIS GAME!!

RIGHT,

LADIES?

THE STRETCH

1. Knees to chest
2. Knees side to side
3. Knees to one side; arms opposite
4. Toe stretch (on a step)
5. Lift weights (3lbs.-5lbs)
6. Standing hip flexor
7. Seated butt stretch
8. Lower back stretches
9. Squats
10. My favorite: Hang onto side of cart and stretch your heels…

There's nothing like a good stretch!

GO

TO

THE

GYM,

STAY

SLIM.

THE PERFECT SWING

I have always had a beautiful
swing; NOT a beautiful score

Just a beautiful swing…..

Why? Why? Why?

No one gave me this clue

IT'S THE SECRET

SPREAD YOUR LEGS,
LADIES!!!

THE STANCE

You heard me……..
No one will give you
this advice.
They will tell you:
"Keep your legs closer(?)"
"Keep your body still   (?)"
"Open your stance   (?)"
"Close your stance   (?)"
SPREAD YOUR LEGS…..

IT WORKS IN EVERY
ROOM!

THE (B) (J)

HERE'S ONE MORE SECRET..

KEEP YOUR HEAD DOWN,
LADIES....

IT

WORKS

IN

GOLF

TOO

THE (T) (I) (T) (S)

(T) TEMPO

(I) IMPROVE

(T) TURN

(S) SWING

THE DRIVER

Get the biggest driver:
One that will give you the longest,
most consistent drive.

DEMO IT.

TRY IT AGAIN.

BELIEVE IN IT………

LOVE

IT

BETTER

THAN

YOUR

LAST

LOVER!

THE PITCH

To pitch:

Feet together,
Cock wrists,
Half swing,
Turn, turn, turn.

To run ball up to the green:

Use a five rescue,
20% of a pitch shot.

IT WORKS!

THE CHIP

Keep your arms straight,
Right to left
Like a pendulum….
Caress it.
Slowly,
Slowly,
Softly,
Softly,
Gentle,
Gentle,
Gentle.
That's it, ladies!

THE SAND

TRY THIS:

Weak grip.

Open club face.

Ball on back foot.

NOW:

Put your legs close together.

Swing through the ball.

DO

NOT

STOP

FOR

ANYTHING!

THE GREENS

HIRE

A

GREAT

CADDY

THE LESSONS

Now, ladies, who listens to us??

Our girlfriends, right??

SOOOOOOOOO......

Who can best understand us?

THE WOMEN PROS.

THINK: My gynocologist of golf.

THINK: My psychiatrist of golf.

THINK: My masseuse of golf.

TRUST THEM:

Women understand you.

Women think like you.

Women are made like you.

IT'S

HOW

WE

THINK,

LADIES.

THE PRACTICE

Take 20 practice shots.

Putt for 10 minutes.

Practice alone once a week:

Use one ball, keep a real score.

Practice alone once a week:

Use many balls; replay bad shots.

Do not keep score.

Play in real games, with real people.

Gain confidence.

Keep trying…..

YOU will get better every week.

I PROMISE!

THE OUTFIT

Now comes the moment of truth….

How old are you?

How short can that skirt be while you still look young and subtle?

At what age does brown spots, face lines, cellulite, gravity and fat ankles overtake your body?

When does reason prevail?

START with those short, short skirts.

START with those tight, tight shirts.

LOVE those traditional saddle shoes with kilties.

BUT as years go by,

As you become an accomplished golfer.

As life takes hold of your mind and body,

"BE REASONABLE",

(my mother always said).

The skirts get longer.

The sleeves get longer.

The shorts get longer.

The pants get longer.

The shirts get bigger.

The hats get bigger.

BUT

So does your golf brain......

All is not lost, girlfriend.

As my mother-in-law said:

"As long as you look good".

Imagine you at the July 4th tournament:

Red, white and blue shirt,

Navy short,

Navy crocodile belt,

Red, white and blue custom shoes,

(Online: $100 extra)

Navy and white hat,

Navy and white socks.

Stand out in the crowd outfit!

HAVE FUN TODAY

HAPPY

INDEPENDENCE

DAY

THE

MOST

FUN

THE MEMBER GUEST

THE CHEATER

NO ONE likes a cheater;

NOT in your home,

OR on the golf course.

DO

NOT

BE

A

CHEATER.

THE MOANER

Okay, ladies. Listen to this:
There is only one room,
 and I mean only one,
That moaning is allowed:
THE BEDROOM
Anywhere else,
It is not respected,
It is not appropriate,
It is not feminine,
It is not adorable.
It is NOT done.

KEEP IT IN THE BEDROOM

THE HYDRATION

A woman of a certain age gets dry,

Right , ladies?

But, we also get dry on the golf course in 90 degree weather.

SO......

Drink lots of water.

Drink tons of sports drinks to replace the electrolytes you lost on the last hole (my personal favorite)

DO NOT EMBARRASS YOURSELF.

DO NOT PASS OUT.

DO NOT GET AIRLIFTED TO THE NEAREST HOSPITAL.

DRINK

DRINK

DRINK

THE CONFIDENCE

Everyone tells us to be confident,

In life and in golf.

But it is not easy.

That comes with age and who wants
to wait?

So go to the course.

Replicate your swing.

TURN
YOUR
RIGHT
HIP,

LIKE
YOU
ARE
DANCING
WITH
YOUR
LOVER.

THE 19TH HOLE

Always plant your feet.

Always spread your legs.

Always have fun.

Oh and…..

Enjoy a margarita

On the 19th hole.

YOU DESERVE IT.

ENJOY GOLF……..

ENJOY

LIFE!

THE END

We all love and hate this game

We all hope for a
breakthrough today.

We love that "aha" moment.

We love that great hole.

We love our day with the girls.

We love the challenge.

We love the 19th hole....

Good luck,ladies!

THE END

HOPEFULLY,
IT
NEVER
ENDS.

19458978R00046

Made in the USA
Middletown, DE
05 December 2018